All That Rhymes With Love

All That Rhymes With Love

A collection of evocative poetry.

ALAN GILBERT

iUniverse, Inc.
New York   Bloomington

All that Rhymes with Love
A Collection of Evocative Poetry

iUniverse books may be ordered through booksellers or by contacting:

iUniverse
1663 Liberty Drive
Bloomington, IN 47403
www.iuniverse.com
1-800-Authors (1-800-288-4677)

ISBN: 978-1-4502-1622-7 (sc)
ISBN: 978-1-4502-1623-4 (ebk)

Library of Congress Control Number: 2010902656

Printed in the United States of America

iUniverse rev. date: 02/26/2010

"All art constantly aspires towards the condition of music."

Walter Pater.

Preface

Poetry is essentially an instantaneous interaction between the author and reader. It has the capacity to evoke the whole range of emotions which make us human. There are many great quotes about poetry. My favorite is, Poetry is the revelation of a feeling that the poet believes to be interior and personal which the reader recognizes as their own, from *Salvatore Quasimodo*.

I have attempted here to produce a selection for a wide range of ages and tastes. The poems have been arranged so there is always something different to discover on the next page. Poetry is an intimate form of communication, producing in the reader an emotional resonance which is born of experience, desire or ambition, whether personal or altruistic. However, as I hope I have demonstrated in this book, sometimes its good just to laugh.

Alan Gilbert, 2010.

For Emy who inspired me to write again.

Contents

Make me a Butterfly.

Make me a butterfly with gossamer wings
Most perfect in form among all living things.
I'd fly round your garden in wind and in rain
Hoping that one day you'd love me again.

Make me a butterfly whiter than snow
And I would fly near you wherever you go.
Perhaps all my dancing would please and there'd be,
Just one word of kindness from your lips for me. .

Make me a butterfly as blue as the sky
I'd fly round the world with a tear in my eye.
And when people asked you why I'm so blue
You'd have to reply it's because I love you.

Make me a butterfly yellow as sand
I'd fly to your table a sit on your hand.
Maybe you'd kiss me and then you would see,
That you could be happy with someone like me.

Make me a Butterfly red as the blood
That surges through veins of all creatures in love.
Is the fate of all butterflies of every hue,
To fall for a heart breaking mayfly like you?

Now only I

I heard a song
That said she waits for you.
I read a poem
That said you would be true.
I felt a breeze
That whispered me your name.
I felt my heart
Surrender when you came.

I close my eyes
And see your smiling face.
I raise my arms
And feel your warm embrace.
I lick my lips
And taste your honey kiss.
I hear my heart
Say *fool* to lose all this.

I walk through trees
Love blossomed as they do.
I see a rose
Less beautiful than you.
I smell the flower
Your fragrance made me reel.
I touch the thorn
The pain I made you feel.

Though time has passed
I'm still drawn to this place.
Where first I saw
The distance in your face.
We were like strangers
Sorrow meeting shame.
A love betrayed
Will never heal again.

Loves senses

Loves colors bright on shining pathways
Whirl round the heart through mind invading hours.
That press my thoughts with prism tinted memories
And soften winter nights with summer flowers.

Loves touch is gentle as the starlight
That falls unceasing through the stillest night.
Yet those caressed will feel it's hidden power
Imbue with joy that heralds reasons flight.

Loves sounds are haunting whispered echoes
Of half remembered words that sought to tell,
The feelings born in those enchanted hours
Of fleeting bliss wherein love cast it's spell.

Loves taste is sweet and bitter intermingled
Each to the other in it's turn must yield.
When sweet reunions fleeting time is ended
Then partings bitter flavour is revealed.

Contradictions

If man's omnipotence brooks no exception
And his desire is measure of its right.
Is progress just a word for self deception
Whilst nurturing the seeds of endless night.

If power aided privilege offers choices
Of only systems that itself ordains.
Is franchisment a means to raise our voices
To argue on the length and weight of chains.

If starving thousands for their daily ration
Only droplets from the fullest cups receive.
Is charity a deeply felt compassion
Or balm to salve the giver not the grieved.

Emily. *A childhood in six short verses.*

Have you seen Emily today
Laughing as she ran to play.
Her hair tied up with ribbons gay.
There's dolls and teddies on display
With Emily today.

Have you seen Emily today
She's quite the tomboy now they say.
Climbs trees and chases boys away
With dares she's just as brave as they
Is Emily today.

Have you seen Emily today
She's found another game to play.
With mouse and visual display
Mails Facebook friends about eBay.
Does Emily today.

Have you seen Emily today
Now growing up the neighbors say.
The world is calling her away
From childhood days that cannot stay,
With Emily today.

Have you seen Emily today
All dressed up and on her way,
To catch a show or see a play.
All heads are turned as if to say
That's Emily today.

I've not seen Emily today.
The house seems sad, she's gone away
To marry in the U.S.A.
New home and friends in Tampa Bay,
No Emily today.

Never drop a hint. *They are fragile!.*

I am sat here drawing breath
But I must put down my pen.
And go to part the curtains
They are squabbling again.
I must go and buy a hammer
As I want to make the bed.
So I went and put the kettle on
But found it hurt my head.

I ought to put the rubbish out
It's been smoldering all day.
But I've gone and broke a promise
And must sweep the bits away.
I was going to beat the carpet
But it's very good at chess.
So I went outside and caught a bus
It was heavy I confess.

She turned around and said
"I was facing the wrong way".
Then we held a conversation
Till it's cares had gone away.
Perhaps I'll wind the clock up
He's very easy to enrage.
Then I found that time was flying
Someone left undone the cage.

If you find you're in a pickle
And can't get out of the jar.
Or while walking on cloud nine
You find you bump into a star.
Perhaps while in a daydream
You find that nights not far away.
Please don't turn into a side street
Because I'd miss you every day.

The whisperers.

Suddenly I'm running
As the path got steeper.
Pushed along by gravity
I find I can't oppose.
My hands and face are torn
By nettle, thorn and creeper.
And darkness hangs upon me
Like a suit of cold wet clothes.

Then I'm thrown into a clearing
Where no living thing would venture.
All around me flesh is rotting
And I'm sickened by the smell.
Then somewhere in the distance
Comes the sound of rolling thunder.
And nearby voices whisper
Saying what, I cannot tell.

Now I'm lying in this putrid place
With terror that consumes me.
My heart is like a hammer
On an anvil deep inside.
The thunder's rolling nearer
With its flashes of fork lightning.
And the voices are still whispering
Saying what, I can't decide.

Now the ground below is trembling
With a roar to match the thunder.
And the lightning strikes come faster
As the storm is overhead.
Then I feel that I am soaking
As the rain has started falling.
And I wake up in a cold sweat
Once more conscious in my bed.

Goodbye Valparaiso.

We were four weeks on our way from Valparaiso,
Sailing home across Atlantic blue.
It's been three years since I kissed you by the harbour,
Long time away
But every day
I thought of you.

We sailed for two weeks more without adventure.
Then as the sun was rising from the sea,
A shout of "Ship ahoy", came from the rigging.
We raised a cheer
To hide our fear
Of piracy.

We stood beside our guns, it seemed an hour.
We watched the corsair drawing ever near.
The skull and crossbones flying from his mainmast,
Nothing was said
By living dead
Our time was here.

We raced toward them both bow chasers blazing.
A lucky chain shot brought their mainsail down.
Then we turned to port, and sunk them with a broadside,
Nothing to do
By we spared few
But watch them drown.

At last we sailed into the English Channel.
We docked at Plymouth on a sunny day.
I promised when I saw you on the quayside,
Now I'm back home
No more I'll roam,
With you I stay.

On hearing of a friend who lost her eyes to glaucoma.

Consider, muse, fantasize.
Not only lose your sight
But lose your eyes.
How would that be?
Never to see
A glimmer of light,
Perpetual night.

What pain. How many tears
Did you endure alone
Yet still so young in years.
Such despair to say
Please give me no more day.
With light and color gone,
Night without dawn.

Eyes that human art has ground
And polished with such care.
Do they reflect the beauty all around?
When sorrow causes tears to flow
Is there that sparkle that I used to know.
Can they smile, as yours were quick to do
And show the world the essence that is you.

A heart in anger.

We're laying here in darkness
And like circles in my head,
I keep playing and rewinding
All the hurtful things you said.
And now you say you're sorry
I believe that's how you feel.
But sorry is a plaster
Over wounds that will not heal.

We've been so long together
And I can't remember when.
Love, became reluctance
To leave and start again.
And so I know we're both to blame
For all that you have said. . .
Sometimes the heart in anger
Betrays truth that's in the head.

Just for a smile.

I thought I'd write a poem
That's different from the rest.
No more love sick Romeo's
Pounding on their breast.
I'd write it in the garden
With just happy thoughts in train.
But when I opened up the door
It was hissing down with rain.

This time I'd set my verses
On a warm and sunny beach.
With bars and cafes all around
And nothing out of reach.
And if the sun got hotter
I'd dive into the sea.
But never say exactly where
That crab got hold of me.

This time my rhyme would be about
The countryside in spring.
With little prancing baby lambs
And swallows on the wing.
We stroll across the meadows
Near the river running by.
Oft gazing at the birds in flight,
Oops! What's that in your eye?

Well that's my little jingle
I hope it made you smile.
I'll try to write another one
In just a little while.
Only now I think its tea time
I've got sandwiches with grouse.
Now think, where did I put those keys?
Oh darn! I'm locked out of the house!

Passion spent.

Another thousand miles
Another thousand years.
However far we travelled
It would always end in tears.

You and me
Meant to be.
Met when passion
Was in fashion.
Thrilling ride
Love inside.
Took the vow
So empty now.
Love? No way
Games we play.
All we share
Neither care.

So now we stare across the void
But neither of us will contend.
Within the joy of each beginning
Is born the sorrow for its end.

Reflections.

I was looking in the mirror
He was looking back at me.
I asked, "Do you know where love is?"
He said, "In everything you see."
I said, "Tell me, where's the reason?"
He replied, "It's in the rhyme."
So I asked, "Where are the answers?"
He said, "They're lost in time."

I was sat alone and talking
To the other one inside.
I said, "There's things I need to tell her,"
He answered, "Lose your foolish pride."
I said, "I never thought she'd hurt me,"
He said, "Everyone's in pain."
I asked, "What if I can't forgive her,?"
He said, "Then, you'll never love again."

I was talking to an echo
He answered every line.
I asked, "Whose words are the wisest?"
He said, "Theirs and yours and mine."
I said, "Tell me where the truth is.?"
He replied, "It's in the lie."
So I asked, "What is our purpose?"
He said, "Be born, love life, then die."

The Fish eyed furry Framper.

Hedgehogs roll up in a ball
Ducks they like to quack.
Tibs sleeps in the garden
With the sunshine on his back.
Dogs enjoy their barking
Lions often pounce.
But the Fish Eyed furry Framper,
All it wants to do is bounce.

I was first into the bathroom
So I washed and combed my hair.
Then went downstairs for breakfast
Sitting in my favorite chair.
I was going back for seconds
When a voice behind me said,
"There's a Fish Eyed furry Framper
Bouncing on your bed".

I was walking in the garden
Just sipping lemonade.
The dog was on the patio
Sleeping in the shade.
When I saw the gardener crying
"What's the matter sir?" I said,
"There's a Fish Eyed furry Framper
Bouncing on the garden shed".

So remember if you're naughty
And go bouncing on your bed.
Trying to touch the ceiling
With the top part of your head.
I'm giving you this warning
Every word I say is true.
You will turn into a Framper
If bounce is what you do!!

Sad spirit of the pool.

I left the city on a summer's day
For just a while I had to get away
From all the noise and traffic of my home
And walk in nature's garden all alone.

Having no idea about my destination,
I caught the first train leaving from the station.
And in a hour or so got off again
In a small village north of Salisbury plain.

I turned and left the village at my back
And wandered down a winding hedge lined track.
I carried on about a country mile
Then to my left I saw a rustic stile.

I crossed the stile and stopped to view the scene
A meadow grassed with nature's deepest green,
That sloped away to blossomed trees below
Which gentle breezes wafted to and fro.

I passed the trees and gasped to see the view
A pool of sparkling water, clear and blue.
Encircled by wild flowers of every kind
The fragrance filled the air and filled my mind.

Weary from my wanderings I did lie
And slept a while, beneath the azure sky.
From this short slumber sudden did I awake
Sensing a movement, from the clear blue lake.

I barely could believe the vision there
With palest skin and longest shining hair.
A slender girl crouched by the pool below
Her flowing dress as white as any snow.

Transfixed I watched this sylph like beauty stand
With crystal droplets falling from her hand.
Which met the dry baked earth and seemed to be
A dappled carpet spread for only she.

While she stood and gazed deep in the pool
A gentle breeze came rippling waters cool.
The sunlight caught her hair that seemed to me
As near to burnished gold as hair could be.

Then melody came floating through the air
Her sweet voice singing echoed everywhere.
Her song so sad as ever could impart
The deepest sorrow to the human heart.

I sat enchanted by her haunting melodies
Until at once the cool wind stirred the trees.
The evening sunlight flickered on her face
I noticed teardrops down her cheeks did race.

I turned away, too hard to see her cry.
When I turned back in a winking of an eye,
That girl had gone. No sight, no sound no trace
Of her was there, though I searched every place.

Now often have I walked that lane since then
But never could I find that place again.
Just once while walking homeward in despair
I thought I heard her singing in the air.

Servants.

We have a maid whose job it is
To keep the whole house clean.
The upstairs and the downstairs
And the landings in between.
But when we're sat relaxing
And she's vacuuming we find,
She'll ask us if we'll lift our feet
But we don't really mind

We have a cook whose job it is
To organize our meals.
She works out in the kitchen
Among potato peels.
And sometimes after dinner
When we're heading for the door,
She asks us if we'll stack our plates
It's really quite a bore.

We have a laundry maid who works
To patch and mend our clothes.
She sees that all the washings done
And hangs it out in rows.
When we rise at nine on Sundays
And she's working at the sink
We're asked to bring our laundry down,
It really makes you think.

Of course you know a well staffed house
Makes for an easy life.
Except that is, for servants
Who are all in fact my wife.
With the washing and the cleaning
And working at the hob.
I'd introduce you but she's out,
She has a part time job!

For Christine.

The sun is setting shining on your face
Now day is calling for the stars to race.
Soon night will hide us, and we'll hear the call
For us to give it up and give it all.
And we will answer as we always do
The world is gone there's only me and you.
Don't ask the question is this right or wrong,
Treasure the moment and be sorry when it's gone.

Now the moon is rising and the sky is clear
My body shakes when you hold me so near.
Then I see my future shining in your eyes
I can't resist although it may be lies.
We know tomorrow wants us back again
We take it slow but still this night will end.
You promise me and I swear to you
We'll be aching for the night the whole day through.

Truly, it's all lies.

Come and sit beside of me
While we are still alone.
There's something I must tell you
Now there's no one else at home.
I've walked a thousand miles
While your journeys hardly planned.
I love you, so I'll lie to you
And hope you understand.

There's no point doing homework
When you'd rather go and play.
Because everything you want from life
Will surely come your way.
As wishing makes things happen
And praying does the same.
But if by chance it all goes wrong
Then the others are to blame.

Never listen to your parents
Because you know what is best.
It's easier to be yourself
Than follow all the rest.
Don't work for good exam results
While you are still at school.
They are only bits of paper
And success is just not cool.

Schoolgirls having children
Is such a clever thing to do.
Babes are quite the fashion item
They help jump the housing queue.
I see them on the High street
Pushing buggies up and down.
It warms the heart for me to see
That all the dads are still around.

Older, bad boys always seem
Exciting and so cool.
They never ever let you down
Well, never as a rule.
Always quick to help you
If trouble comes your way.
To love you and support you
And the children every day.

If you're lucky you can marry
Then he'll quickly change his ways.
He'll stop drinking or injecting
And the other games he plays.
So when he loses patience
And starts beating you, just say,
I know he really loves me
He's said sorry anyway.

I'm glad of these few minutes
To have a chat with you.
Just remember that before this verse
Not a word of it was true.
The last thing that I want to say
As I put down my pen.
I promise that I'll never,
Ever lie to you again.

The secret glade

On such a day in summer season's height
When all the world was bathed in colors bright.
With fiery orb in azure skies above
This woodland glade bore witness to our love.

We held this place as secret though I'm sure
That other loves have walked this way before.
And tasted first the magic that will come
When hearts and minds and bodies merge as one.

Since then in bitter winds we've walked this way
When skies and summer colors fade to grey.
We share a glance and feel our pulses race
Remembering still that summer's sweet disgrace.

Vermin.

See another hunt is meeting
On the green below the lane.
Some protesters have gathered
But of course they're quite insane.
Fox hunting is traditional
Conservancy what's more.
A quick, clean kill of vermin
That's what the hunt is for.

See the huntsmen dressed in scarlet
Spring nimbly from the ground.
Sitting upright in the saddle
As they pass the cup around.
The loud shrill horn is sounded
As they drain the stirrup clean.
A quick, clean kill of vermin
That's what the huntsmen mean.

See the fox has broken cover
And the race for life is on.
They blocked the hole below the dyke
Its only hope is gone.
The panic stricken headlong chase
Is all to no avail.
It's a quick, clean kill of vermin
And the hounds are on the trail.

See the fox sprint for the thicket
Racing high above the downs.
See not twenty yards behind it
Run a pack of yelping hounds.
Hear the chilling screams of terror
As flesh from bone is rent
A quick, clean kill of vermin
Is this what the huntsmen meant?

A child in time.

I heard that someone wrote a poem
More than a thousand years ago.
The author isn't mentioned
So I guess we'll never know.
Found at an excavation
In the land of Palestine.
It talks about a child
Who was thought to be divine.

It says there was a baby
Delivered in a darkened place.
The world seemed to be brightened
By the smile upon his face.
It says his eyes were open wide
And of the deepest blue.
And it says they held a promise
Of hope for me and you.

It seems the babies crying
Was heard by passersby.
And because it seemed so out of place
They went to find out why.
Some of them carried presents
It doesn't mention what they were.
But reminds me of a story
Of gold, frankincense and myrrh.

It doesn't say the mother's name
But maybe that's because,
It implies that there were rumors
As to whom the father was.
Reports by those that held him
Said there was calmness in his eyes.
And they got the strangest feeling
That this new born babe was wise.

That's all I have to tell you
I wish that there was more.
I want to know what happened next
What all the fuss was for.
Some scholars say he's just a child
That time has left behind.
But many think this gentle babe
Was the savior of mankind.

Eternity

Oh who has walked on hills or heard the rages
Of windswept oceans tear at rock strewn shore.
And heard the voice that speaks of endless ages
Before our time and when we are no more.

Though mans existence seems to be forever
It starts and ends as lightning's earthbound race.
Ten thousand pages filled with bold endeavor
Will ebb away and leave no single trace.

Yet still we run toward the final slaughter
As mad men who feel righteous in their crime.
But man's demise will barely move the water
A silent ripple on the calm of time.

So know proud man with all your seeming power
Through endless ages all your works are just
A single second in times endless hour
A simple thought, that will return to dust.

The death of Eos.

Once while early days recalling
Back through years my mind was falling.
Back to fond remembered schooldays
When the world seemed like a friend.

All at once this boy was walking
Through that boarding school, and talking
To those friends from distant memory
Of things that seemed to matter then.

The flying Scot and other trains
Comic books and fighter planes.
All the things that young minds dwell on,
Not at least the senior girls.

One of these with perfect form
Eos, goddess of the dawn.
Her smile like the sweetest arrow
Pierced the hearts of all that saw.

A burning beauty such as she
Born to fulfill her destiny.
Of worldwide travel, gems and cars,
Leaving us in public bars.

Back to the present flew my mind
I'd find those friends I left behind.
Meet this beauty just to see
If dream became reality.

Through computer data bases
I discovered schooldays faces.
And from one the fates bestowed
Eos's number, home and code. .

Nervous with anticipation
I took the handset from its station.
Punched the number, heard the tone
Ringing in some distant home.

The voice that answered, old and hollow
Told me of a life of sorrow.
Of such pain and tribulation
As to break the strongest will.

More than this, there seemed to be
No trace of personality.
No confidence or love of life
No glamour, just a tale of strife.

I had imagined for her life
Beauty, pleasure, mother, wife.
Just a young boy's fantasy
Devoid of harsh reality.

Putting down the phone I cried
For something missing now inside.
A whisper deep inside me said
Mourn if you will, Eos is dead.

The child's heart.

I'm sorry when I met you first
That I was someone else.
The child that I was then
Just couldn't see.
To lose a love through silence
Is the saddest thing of all.
I wish we could have met
When I was me.

I'm sorry when I saw you first
It was through a child's eyes.
Eyes so dull it seems
They didn't know.
If you become distracted
Then beauty slips away.
That beauty now these eyes
Will never know.

I'm sorry when I loved you first
It was with a child's heart.
A heart believing wishes
Make things so.
Although that child wanted
What the man is missing now.
The man's heart would have
Never let you go.

What is left.

You ask me if I love you
Do the seasons run on time.
Are the sun and moon rotating
Are there poets left to rhyme.
Is the tide ebbing and flowing
Does summer follow spring,
Are the wild flowers blooming
Are there songbirds left to sing.

Does the smile of a baby
Still thaw the coolest heart.
Do lovers keep on yearning
Every time they are apart.
To answer any question
Is so easy when it's true.
When all these things have ended
What is left is, I love you.

Unspoken Love.

Are you looking at this glowing moon like me
In you're not so distant home across the sea.
If thoughts were free to travel fast as light
You'd know how much I'm missing you tonight.

Yes, I know the promise that I made
But sometimes by our hearts we are betrayed.
My heart says it's a foolish thing to do
To spend each waking hour in thoughts of you.

I feel detached as though I walk on air,
Although you're gone I seek you everywhere.
You're out of reach yet still I feel your touch.
I'm young again because I love so much.

I close my eyes and summon up your face.
Which makes me sad; I'm just a hopeless case.
I think maybe you'd smile if you knew
How constantly my body aches for you.

I sit and write a letter every day
Pouring out the things I long to say.
But courage fails and so I start again
And ramble on about long queues and rain.

Now my true feelings you may never know
As mundane letters travel two and fro.
Sometimes my heart will whisper, could it be,
You lay awake and spend your nights with me?

A lover's moon.

A girl and boy came walking
When a lover's moon was high.
A thousand stars were shining
The breeze was warm and dry.
They shared the many secrets
Young lovers always do.
When nothing stands between them
And all their world is new.

She sighs and leans against him
But doesn't understand,
Why his body starts to tremble
When she reaches for his hand.
He too is lost in wonder
Why his heart begins to race,
When he gazes at her beauty
With the moonlight on her face.

The path led to a coppice
Was there magic in that place?
Or was it just on impulse
They shared that long embrace.
And there they lay enraptured
As **passion's** always bloom.
When boy and girl go walking
Beneath a lover's moon.

Up a tree?.

Two cats are sitting in a tree.
One said, "You are more wise than me;
Would you tell me, make it clear,
How do we get down from here?"

"The question is," the wise one said
Leaning back to scratch his head.
"If we just stepped off would we fall,
Are we two in a tree at all?"

The first one said while looking round,
"The sky is up the earth is down.
It seems so obvious to me
That we two cats are in a tree."

"You think that's so the other said
"But you try standing on your head.
The earth is up the sky is down
And not the other way around."

He replied, " But don't you see
The leaves that fall past you and me.
Are falling past from sky to ground
So we two can't be upside down."

"Ah yes but don't be fooled by that
You sleep as well as any cat.
So things may not be as they seem
All of this could be a dream!"

The first one purred and said, " I see
Of course we are not up a tree."
With that he stepped off of the bough,
He fell and landed on a cow!

What love wants.

Love wants to walk beside you
And talk just like a friend.
Or give you nights of passion
You wish would never end.
It never makes you guilty
For things that you have done.
Love wants you to remember
That it's nothing if not fun.

Love wants to raise your spirits
When the worlds too much to bear.
It will make your heart feel empty
When you wake and it's not there.
But when you're back together
And the spark becomes a flame.
Love wants you both to promise
That you'll never part again.

Love wants you to think with your heart
And seldom with your head.
You won't need pen and paper
When you're snuggling in bed.
You can find love anywhere
So you shouldn't be surprised.
Love wants to sometimes smile at you
From someone else's eyes.

Love wants to be a captive
And sometimes to be free.
You cannot hold it hostage
You just have to let it be.
So when your heart is broken
And you feel you'll love no more.
Love wants to come and visit
So never lock the door.

Lost.

To the edge, empty, baron as the cold
Grey featureless ocean upon which I gaze.
Lost, again say lost, in the pointless
Futility of my own existence.
Now her voice comes to me
Carried on the cold harsh wind.
It surrounds and invades me.
Now here now there, now soft now loud
Now caressing now reproaching.
Waxing and waning as Selene's eternal round.

"When was that time, hour, moment,
In which our hearts diverged.
When we together desolate
Thought the other to be distant
What thought you then.
That I above all would be the betrayer
Of each gentle kiss, each impassioned act
Of our most indulgent lust,
Which we in our innocent days
Had gathered sacred to ourselves?

Did you then suppose
To shed all that we were,
To think, abandoned by my love
To strike down in the coldest blood
All that we had been, could have been.
Where were they then, those words
That once sprang eager from our lips
When we in closest harmony shared all?
Yet we honing our words to sharpest edge,
Inflicting wound on wound.

I never loved but you. Such love
That echoed through my dreams,
Soul and soul in perfect congress.
Yet hurt on cursed hurt
Condemned us to oblivion.
Our precious, dearest love
Benighted by we two alone
Starved by our mutual neglect.
Lost, forever and forever lost."
One step…..

Just two years.

"It's cancer I'm afraid" she said
Sitting at the foot of bed.
"It's in your bones and so you see
In two years you will cease to be".
Just two years.

"Of course that's an approximation
With treatment your prostate inflation
Will subside and you will see,
You'll walk and dance as well as me."
For just two years.

I smiled, I really don't know why
It seemed more stoic than to cry.
I lay back down and watched her go
And wished to God I didn't know about
Just two years.

I lay awake and counted out
All of those I cared about.
But found that unlike jumping sheep
This adding would not help me sleep
Until two years.

And now I'm living in denial.
When it's said I have to smile.
For it's a lovely place to be
I know that it has set me free for,
Just two years.

When did you last

When did you last run down a beach
Then in the sea run back again.
Or make love through the afternoon
Calling service for champagne.
Or sip Chianti through the night
Talking until half past two.
Or just look in the mirror knowing
That you've kept some love for you.

When did you last eat candy floss
And found it sticking to your nose.
Or play that game of poker
Where the loser sheds their cloths.
Or stood admiring birds in flight
The Eagle soar the Swallow dive.
Or wake up in the morning thinking
How good it is to be alive.

Reste der schwärzesten Nacht

Embalmed in vaults and archives
Lay memories time and webs encrust.
Though years decay vague visions stay
Of hate and love and lust.
And all the while the crazed machine
That breaks our will and mills to dust
The soul that night has fought to keep
From razor chains defiled by rust.

So formed the thought that spawned the deed
Which raged against creations need.
To curse in blood forever more
And procreated bitter seed.
In wretched form the issue stood
Bereft of feelings, bad nor good,
To face alone the vengeful wrath
Of gaping wounds that cried, "Enough".

Time

Time was not my enemy
Neither was it friend.
Time is never constant
And seldom does it mend.
When I had time to wander
I wanted time to settle down.
But time just made me restless
And kept turning me around.

There once was time to think about
Things that I would do.
There was time to be with others
There was time to spend with you.
And now when time is precious
Too late it's made me see.
That if I'd spent time more wisely
You and I could still be, we.

Savage love.

The wizened elf
That stamps as time dilates.
Forced by midnights hour
On she who hates.
The thunderstorm clouds pass
Yet darkness stays
To hide the clown
Who penance never pays.

Chained by savage
Razor links that rust.
They tear at wounds
Inflicted by her lust.
The plunging knife
And dreadful searing heat.
Turned black the heart
That echoed our defeat.

My addiction.

I went to see my doctor
I have this pain inside.
When other folks are sleeping
My eyes are open wide.
I never eat my dinner
So now I just don't cook.
People say I'm in a daze
And have a distant look.

He gave his diagnosis
He said that in his view.
I have a strong addiction
The cause of which is you.
He said it's very common
He knows the symptoms well.
Though I'm the worst case that he's seen
Just why he couldn't tell.

So now I hope you understand
What I've been going through.
Now I have a prescription
For a daily dose of you.
The cure is as simple
As one and one are two.
The only sum we need is
One is me and you.

May dreams restore.

Walking on the crossing
Guide dog at her feet.
Frail and bent by times unyielding hand.
Her face seems old and careworn
Where a smile seldom shows.
Who she was, no one can understand.

Who knew her in those golden years
When she was sixteen summers old.
Full of sparkle, life without a care.
Her face would shame a goddess
Her form delight the eye
Amazing beauty envied everywhere.

She moved with casual confidence
Born of a knowing heart.
Her intellect as sharp as all her peers.
Her gentle sense of humour
That brought a smile to her lips.
Crushed by her misfortune over years.

I pray that when she sleeps at night
She's taken to that place.
Where dreamers go
And are at peace once more.
If I had a wish, it would surely be
The joy of life she knew may dreams restore.

Now put away.

Now put away the glittering balls
The holly that bedecked the halls.
Tree the children loved to dress
Now dropping needles, what a mess.
Cards from friends both far and near
You'll hear from them again, next year..
The mistletoe now looking sad
That was so fresh when Mum kissed Dad.

Put the fairy lights away
That shone so bright on Christmas day.
Tags and wrapping paper please
Recycle them to save the trees.
Put the fairy back to bed
A year to rest her pretty head.
But keep the peace on earth and cheer
You may need them throughout New Year.

Alzheimer's. Sneak thief of the mind.

Stealthy as a sneak thief it creeps into his head.
It starts with," senior moments." as they say.
With no pain or other symptoms, there is no sign at all.
But gradually it steals his mind away.

Slowly he's forgetting all the things he meant to do,
He climbs the steps and wanders why he's there.
Yet still he can remember all those far off childhood days,
So no one thinks that there's a cause for care.

Then people start to realize there's really something wrong.
He doesn't recognize them when they call.
As if some friends and family had been airbrushed from his life,
To him they never did exist at all.

And now he's in a special place and still no symptom shows.
Nobody comes to visit, well, nobody that he knows.
A lady called this morning, but soon she left in tears
He never even recognized his wife of thirty years.

One day she gets a phone call from the nursing home.
Her husband died this morning, eleven thirty, all alone.
She put down the receiver, then sitting down she cried,
Tears for her late husband, for the second time he died.

Whatever.

"What would you like from us for Christmas dear?"
"Whatever."
"We thought something more grown up this year."
"Whatever."
"Your father thought you'd maybe like a bike."
Whatever.
Or you could have some makeup if you like.
Whatever.
A dress, a watch, a bracelet or a hat.
A broach, a tattoo, camera, or a cat.
W h a t e v e r!
A hair do, pony, ear rings or a car.
A flat, a house, New Hampshire or a star!
WHATEVER!

Good morning Mother on this Christmas day.
Where are my presents, are they hid away?
I know you sometimes like to have your fun,
I'm starting to believe you've bought me *none*!

WHATEVER!!

Fred.

I glanced back at the telly
The adverts had come on.
"Please help us save the polar bears
Before the last is gone.
Just send us fifty dollars
And we will send to you,
A certificate of adoption
And photograph or two.

I thought it was a pity
If these fine beasts should go.
If all the ice caps melted
Global warming don't you know.
So I sent off my remittance
And it happened as they said,
They sent a form of adoption
My own bears name was Fred.

You know it made me feel so good
To think what I had done.
If all the others perished
I had a least saved one.
Imagine my amassment
When answering my bell.
My polar bear was at the door,
With smile and trunk as well.

He came right in and settled down
In my favorite easy chair.
He looked around as if to say
Have you any fish to spare.
I went into the kitchen
But all I had was cake.
But Fred just growled at me,
This was my first mistake.

So then I went out shopping.
I thought just to be kind
I'd take Fred along with me,
Instead of leaving him behind.
We went into the market
To buy some fish for tea,
But then Fred let go of my hand
And ran away from me.

I found Fred in a while
Eating fish off of a stall.
He didn't wear a napkin
He just didn't care at all.
I told the man "I'm sorry,
He just doesn't understand."
It only cost me thirty dollars,
Adopting polar bears is grand!

Now Fred's been here a while
Really made himself at home.
He doesn't care to shower
Wash his face or use a comb.
So if you're feeling lonely
And want to stay in bed.
No need to send me money,
For free I'll send you....Fred.

Funny love.

Did you ever stop to wonder
What a funny thing is love.
We call each other fluffkins
Ichycoo or Turtle dove.
When whispering sweet nothings
Into your loved ones ear,
Who would think that nothing
Was such a thrilling thing to hear.

Not something I'd disparage
But I'll say it anyway.
It's romantic writing letters
To someone you see every day.
Now you'll think me old fashioned
And say, "Whatever next."
But I really think it's careless
If you only send a text.

If you pay to see a movie
You'll be really glad you came.
Because when the pictures over
You won't have seen a single frame.
Though love can be amusing
I would not change it if I could.
Of all the things you'll find in life
There's nothing half as good.

Love speaks.

Love speaks and those who listen
Are helpless to resist.
It tells of what their missing
Those who never have been kissed.
Who've never watched a lover
Sleeping in their arms,
Or had the other tell them
How they're weakened by their charms.

It says that if you search for love
It seldom comes your way.
But when you least expect it
Love creeps up on you one day.
And then it overwhelms you
It's the greatest thing of all,
It really will amaze you
How far a heart can fall.

So be certain that you're listening
In case love speaks to you.
It doesn't give instruction
Or tell you what to do.
It's way is sweet seduction
And seldom will you find.
That listeners will ignore it
And put love out of their mind.

The social network.

I really love to log onto my social network site.
I find that I am chatting well into the night.
The prompt will always tell me exactly who's on line
The girl I "met" this morning, long term friends of mine.
Choose status line with comment or instant messaging,
It doesn't really matter, communication that's the thing.

Just type into the text box, check the spelling then hit "share."
It only takes you seconds to reach people anywhere.
Our cousin in Vancouver, my brother down the street,
No one need be out of touch, community complete.

Now I'm sitting here just thinking, I've not logged on today.
About my next door neighbor who lived twenty yards away.
Police have just come to my door; I was shaken when they said,
This frail and lonely woman, found this morning three days dead.

All that rhymes with love.

If all uplifting music
Was heard by everyone.
And all love verse ever written
Sprang easy from each tongue.
If all denizens of power
Oppressors of the weak.
Could only utter what is true
Each time they tried to speak.
If all the lost and lonely souls
Could take another's hand.
If the rich admit there's plenty
To be shared by every land.
If all these things could happen
I swear by stars above,
That every poet's heart would fill with
All that rhymes with love.

About the author.

Born in Southampton, England, Alan Gilbert attended the West of England School and St Lloys College Exeter. He took his degree in psychology and art at The Open University, graduating in 1984. Alan and his wife, Barbara, have three grown children. He lives in Southampton.